ROCK CURRICULUM
FOUNDATIONS OF ROCK: GUITAR RIFFS IN THE STYLE OF THE 60s & 70s
BY JON FINN
Mel Bay Guitar University Series

CD contents —— Jon Finn – Guitar • David Buda – Bass • Larry Finn – Drums ——

1 Tuning	16 Tubing! – no guitar	30 Lift Your Head Higher – guitar only
2 Twist Little Bamba - full	17 Over at the Intersection – full	31 Lift Your Head Higher – no guitar
3 Twist Little Bamba - guitar only	18 Over at the Intersection – guitar 1 only	32 Shallow Violet – full
4 Twist Little Bamba - no guitar	19 Over at the Intersection – guitar 2 only	33 Shallow Violet – guitar only
5 Secret Aging Man – full	20 Over at the Intersection – no guitar 1	34 Shallow Violet – no guitar
6 Secret Aging Man – guitar only	21 Over at the Intersection – no guitar 2	35 Giving You the Business – full
7 Secret Aging Man – no guitar	22 Over at the Intersection – no guitar	36 Giving You the Business – guitar 1 only
8 House of the Morning Sun – full	23 It's Getting Near Don – full	37 Giving You the Business – guitar 2 only
9 House of the Morning Sun – guitar only	24 It's Getting Near Don – guitar only	38 Giving You the Business – no guitar 1
10 House of the Morning Sun – no guitar	25 It's Getting Near Don – no guitar	39 Giving You the Business – no guitar 2
11 Tubing! – full	26 More Cowbell – full	40 Giving You the Business – no guitar
12 Tubing! – guitar 1 only	27 More Cowbell – guitar only	41 Sour Condo in Pittsburgh – full
13 Tubing! – guitar 2 only	28 More Cowbell – no guitar	42 Sour Condo in Pittsburgh – guitar only
14 Tubing! – no guitar 1	29 Lift Your Head Higher – full	43 Sour Condo in Pittsburgh – no Guitar
15 Tubing! – no guitar 2		

With the purchase of this book/2-DVD set, free companion audio MP3 example and back-up tracks are available for download at www.melbay.com/mp3/20999CD. Play-along with a back-up band or hear the guitar part played slowly and at tempo. These MP3 files are free to download and store on your computer.

1 2 3 4 5 6 7 8 9 0

Visit us on the Web at www.melbay.com — E-mail us at email@melbay.com

Table of Contents

Acknowledgements

Ibanez guitars, Laney Amplifiers, Berklee College of Music, Boston Symphony Orchestra, my family, Patti Hanscom, Paul Behringer, Charlie Hollis, Joe Santerre, Larry Finn, Ross Ramsay, David Buda

Introduction

Much of the Language of Rock Guitar is in riffs. A riff is a short musical phrase that is repeated enough to serve as a "signature" inside of a song. Riffs are the part we play when we do "Air Guitar" to our favorite tunes! Riffs are what made me want to play guitar. They are fun, usually pretty easy to play and they sound great.

After I learned the basics of how to play from a teacher (a few chords and some strum patterns), my next phase was learning riffs. These days I spend a lot of time exploring the finer points of Rock Guitar. That means analyzing obsessively, practicing constantly, listening, transcribing, studying and writing. I do this because I love to play guitar and I want to be as good at it as I can possibly be. When I started I wanted to have fun and sound good. I played riffs to have fun (I still do, actually). Because it was fun, I did it a lot. Because I did it a lot, I got good at it. I thought that I was doing it "wrong" because I never felt like I was "in school." Many guitarists I've spoken to seem to feel the same way: Riffs are a guilty pleasure when we're practicing.

Riffs are the cornerstone of Rock Guitar as it turns out. A guitarist of average ability learning to play riffs can be playing in a band and sounding pretty darn good within one year.

Many guitarists have asked me what the "right" way to learn guitar is. Their concern seems to be that they don't want to learn something only to unlearn it later (which is something I've had to do many times!). I've often wondered if I could have saved myself years of heartache if I got it right the first time.

What I think today is that we learn what we need to learn when we're ready to learn it. Therefore, there is no single linear path to the "right" way to play guitar. We get better by playing a lot. We get better when we start asking ourselves why something we've been playing sounds a certain way. But first we have to notice those finer points. I didn't practice scales, arpeggios, reading and all of those "good for your discipline" elements of musicianship until it became clear that I would not progress without it.

With that in mind, we bring you "Riffs Volume One." It is a collection of riffs that will serve as a great introduction to 60's and 70's era Rock Guitar. These were chosen because they are all pretty easy to play and they sound good. I had a lot of fun putting it together.

If you're planning to make Rock Guitar a lifetime commitment, learn riffs. If you're simply looking for a way to have fun in your spare time, learn riffs. All roads really do lead to Rome! If you're having fun, you're doing it right!

How to Use this Book

You will need these items:

-Your guitar, cable, amplifier and a pick.
-Music stand (A tabletop will suffice but I like the music stand better.)
-Guitar tuner
-Pencil (to write notes to yourself in the music)
-This book
-A CD player

Always start each practice session by tuning up. Never assume your guitar is in tune. It only takes a moment to tune. Doing so will guarantee your guitar will sound better. If it sounds better, you'll like it more. If you like it more, you'll probably play more because it's fun. That's what we're after right? Fun?

Next, set your amp to the desired volume and tone settings. Work on getting the best sound possible from the equipment you're using. Try to avoid practicing without the guitar connected to the amp. Remember, since the amp has a big influence on your tone, it is part of your musical instrument.

Set the book on your music stand and the CD player within arm's reach. Keep the pencil on the music stand. Each example in the book will tell you which CD tracks to look for, and what is actually on the track. Lastly, balance the volume of your amp to your CD player so you can hear both clearly while you play.

<u>The Music Notation:</u>

In each example, you will see tips on tone and technique (including a diagram that shows suggested amp settings you can try), standard musical notation, fret-hand fingerings (*next* to the notes on the standard notation staff), picking and strum marking (*above* the notes in the standard notation staff), articulation markings (*below* the notes in the standard notation staff), tablature, chord diagrams and other assorted marking that might help. Since not everyone learns in quite the same way, you are encouraged to pick through (no pun intended) the information you think will be most helpful and put the rest aside until it becomes useful.

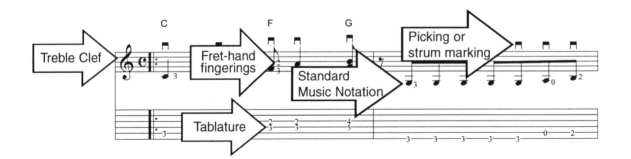

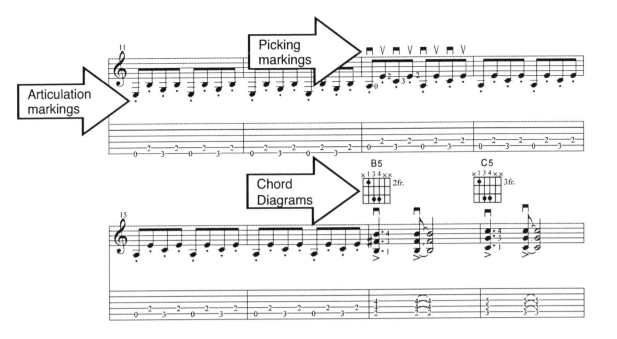

The CD

Most of the time, you will get each example presented like this on the CD:

-The riff played with the backing tracks (bass, drums, keyboards and percussion if any) in its entirety

-Only the guitar part, so you can hear what you're supposed to play by itself.

-Only the Backing tracks, so you can play your part with the backing tracks

-Backing tracks plus Guitar 2 (if there are two guitar parts) so you can play Guitar 1 along with the tracks

-Backing tracks plus Guitar 1 (if there are two guitar parts) so you can play Guitar 2 along with the tracks

Once you get everything set up in this way, look over the music itself. If all this information is too overwhelming, then use the information that makes sense to you and ignore the rest for now. Some of us will use the tab first, while others may read the music. Still others may ignore the music notation and simply learn by ear. Any of these approaches are perfectly valid.

Twist Little Bamba

Tips on playing this riff

Tone:

This is the classic early 60's "twist" sound. To me the only difference between that and the "surf" guitar sound is that it uses just a little less reverb. Though you don't add any overdrive, picking the notes hard will produce an edgy "honk" to the notes as you play them. Use the guitar's bridge pickup and pick closer to the bridge than normal.

On your amp, start with a basic clean sound. Set your bass to "4", middle to "6" and treble to "5" as shown in the graphic below. Add a moderate amount of reverb. Leave the "bright" switch off because picking closer to the bridge will sharpen the tone enough. Adding the "bright" switch might give it a sound that's too "icy." Try it for yourself and see.

Technique:

Playing this piece is a mix of arpeggios (chords played one note at a time) and double-stops (pairs of notes played together). Listen to the example a few times, then play it again. Follow the fingerings and pickings as indicated.

You will see that the music shows the chord symbol, but not the chord diagram. You don't ever play the whole chord at any time, but you do play some of it.

Once you get this to where you can play it in tempo with the recording, practice putting a little bit of space (by lifting your fret-hand fingers off the fretboard just slightly). This will make each note "bounce" a little more. As with all the examples, listen closely to what comes out of your amp. Compare it to the recording. Go with what you think sounds good.

Music:

Note that the music has "repeat" signs, plus a first and second ending. Follow the directions indicated. Play measures 1-8, then go back to the beginning. Next, play measures 1-7. Skip over measure 8 and play measure 9 instead.

Twist Little Bamba

Play this measure, then go back to the beginning.

On the 2nd time, skip the 1st ending,
and play this instead.

Secret Aging Man
Tips on playing this riff

Tone:

This one requires a tone that can only be described as "gnarly". Set your guitar's pickup selector to it's bridge pickup and turn your volume and tone knobs to "10". Set your amp to a clean tone. Leave your "bright" switch off because you probably won't need it. Experiment with your "bass", "middle" and "treble" knobs. The settings shown here are the ones I used on my amp, but every setup will sound a little different. Originally, I had the "bright" switch on, but it was too obnoxious sounding. By leaving it off, and picking closer to the bridge, I got the sound I was looking for. Dial in a generous dose of reverb ("4" or "5" if you like). You may find that if the sound is "too clean" (not gnarly enough), than you may want to experiment with adding a small amount of overdrive. Be careful! Too much overdrive will be worse than not enough. You want a clean sound with just a hint of overdrive. Since mine is a tube amp, it distorts just a little bit if you hit the strings hard.

Technique:

Here you have to hold all the notes of the chord as long as you can. Strum the whole chord (all six strings at once using a downstroke) at the beginning of each phrase as indicated. Next, pick the high notes while the rest of the notes are still ringing. The notes on the top strings should ring in to each other. If they don't, maybe fret-hand fingers need to stand up more. For example: If your first finger is holding the first fret on the B string, it should stand up enough so that the high E string can ring clearly too. It takes practice to get that going. I find that it helps a great deal to pay attention to my posture. If I am sitting or standing in a way that's comfortable, I can usually reach better, and play for longer periods. If I can practice longer without getting tired, I get better faster, and I enjoy it more because fatigue is less of an issue.

Secret Aging Man

This page has been left blank to avoid awkward page turns.

House of the Morning Sun
Tips on playing this riff

Tone:

Set your amp to a clean, bright tone. Don't forget to add liberal amounts of reverb for that funky sixties "surf/pop" sound. Set your guitar's pickup selector to its "bridge" pickup setting. Turn your guitar's volume and tone knobs up to "10". Picking closer to the bridge will accentuate the "twang" effect.

Technique:

Use your pick to attack every note. Some teachers and players may recommend using an alternate picking technique (where you alternately pick "down, up, down, up etc."), but I am not at all certain it's necessary. Pick each string evenly and make sure all the notes ring. Do it whichever way feels most comfortable to you. Listen closely to the sound you make. If it sounds right, it probably is.

Your fret-hand can benefit a great deal from what I call "prepatory" fingering. As you can see, each measure of music is one chord arpeggiated (played one note at a time). It looks like you have to change all your fingers all at once. There are several places where only one finger has to move to get the next note. This makes it much easier. When practicing, you'll find that notes in one measure lead you right to the next measure smoothly. It's important to think in "phrases" rather than "measures." Remember, the measures are like mile markers on a road, telling you where you are. Don't make the mistake of practicing in a way that uses measure lines as temporary stopping points. This tends to chop up the music in a way that makes it unrecognizable.

House of the Morning Sun

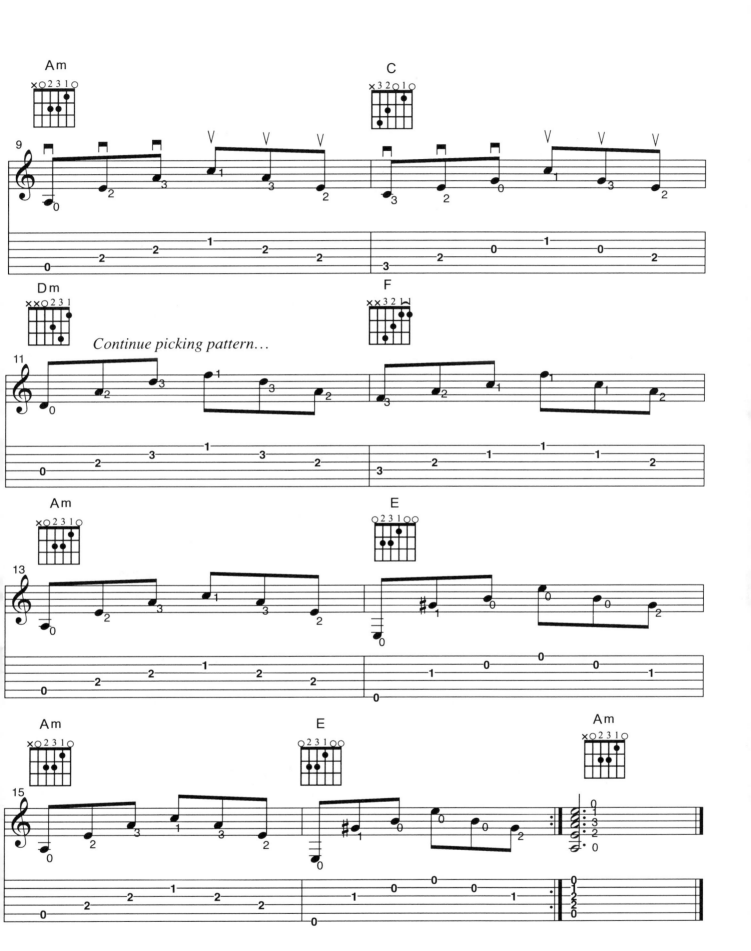

Continue picking pattern…

Tubing! - Guitar 1
Tips on playing this riff

Tone:

If your name is Franky (or Sonny, or maybe even Dash), your best friend is referred to as Moondoggy, your girl's name is Susie, Ginger, Annette (but not Gidget), and your life's passion is in pursuit of "The Big Kahuna", then you will have no trouble being able to conceptualize this sound. For the rest of us, we can put on sunglasses, loud Hawaiian shirts, sandals, shorts and a healthy dose of sunblock, but only on our noses.

For the Guitar 1 part, use the bridge pickup and turn your volume and tone controls all the way up to "10". If you want less volume, turn down your amp, but leave your guitar's volume up. Most electric guitars have a strange tendency to change the tone when you use the guitar's volume knob. Usually it gets darker sounding. I am not totally sure why this happens but it does. I use the guitar's volume knob for one of two reasons:

-I want to turn down and I don't mind the change in sound.

-If I want less overdrive or distortion in my guitar sound.

Set your amp for a clean sound and start with your bass, middle and treble controls set to around "5" (or their middle point, wherever that is), then adjust to your own taste. Use the "bright" switch on your amp if it has one. Dial in generous amounts of reverb.

Technique:

There are 3 parts to this riff:

-The low 8th notes.

-The "Power chords".

-The Turnaround (the last phrase which takes you back to the beginning).

Let's look at each.

The Low 8th notes:
Lean your pick-hand palm against the low strings just enough so that the note still sounds, but goes "thunk" instead of it's normal sound. This is called "palm muting." Back in the old days, some guitars were built with a felt muting device with a lever that would swing the device out of the way when not in use. It rarely worked! Anyway, pick as close to the bridge as possible, making sure your palm can still properly mute the strings.

The "Power chords":
Each chord only uses strings 5(A), 4(D), and 3(G) so you have to be very careful to pick only those strings. Using a downstroke on each chord, place the pick slightly above the 5th (A) string (or described a different way, between the 6th (E) string and the 5th (A) string). Strum past the 3rd (G) string and use the 2nd (B) string to stop your pick. Think of the 2nd (B) string as a row of kids in a game of "Red Rover" stopping the kid who's "IT." Doing this properly insures you play just the right number of notes in each chord.

The Turnaround:
A turnaround is a musical phrase that is often used as a form of punctuation. Turnarounds are used a lot in Blues (for that matter in many other forms too!). In this case the turnaround comes after the "Power Chords." Playing this properly is a way of saying, "Here we go back to the beginning!" Play this in the same way as the "low 8th notes" but make sure you are not muting. You want the Turnaround to sound different from the "low 8th notes."

Tubing! - Guitar 1

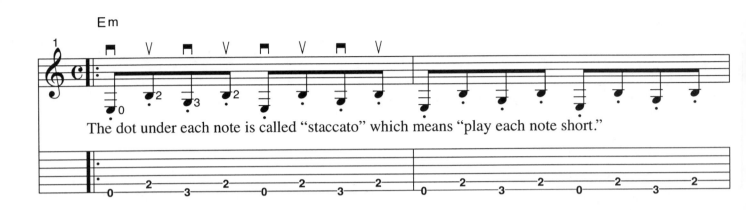

The dot under each note is called "staccato" which means "play each note short."

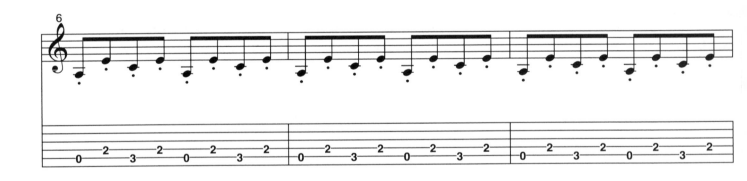

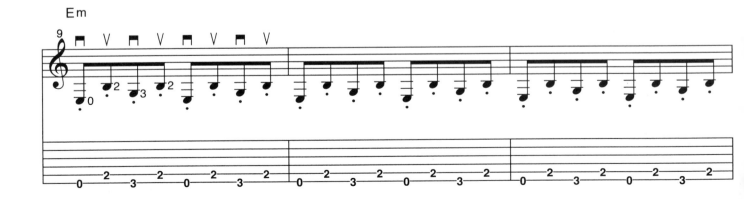

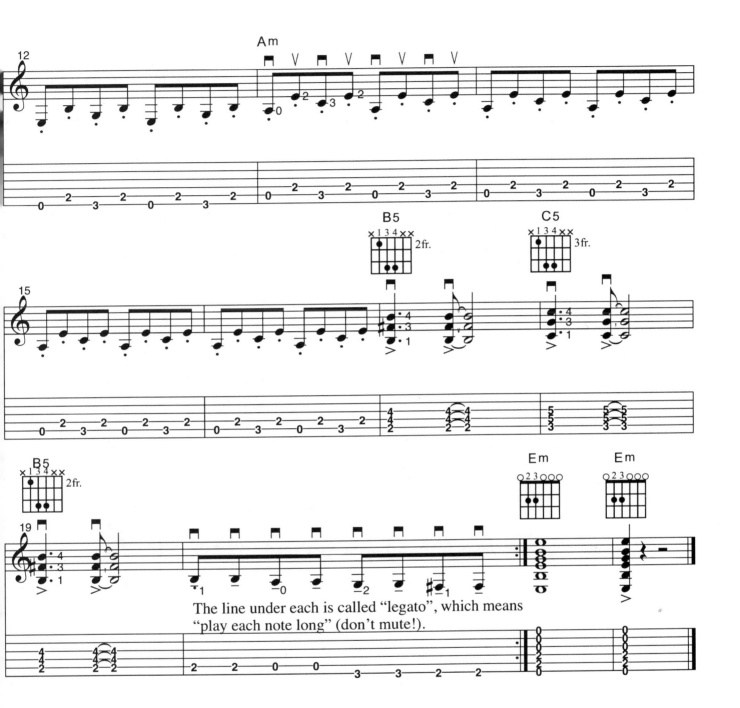

The line under each is called "legato", which means "play each note long" (don't mute!).

Tubing! - Guitar 2

Tips on playing this riff

Tone:

Because this part is played with guitar 1, it's a good idea to set the sound so that it blends with the other part, but does not conflict with it. Guitar 1 uses a bright and aggressive sound playing in the lower register. Guitar 2 plays the melody using a similar (but not quite the same) sound.

Use the bridge + middle pickup setting (or bridge+neck if you prefer). Set your volume to "10", but set your tone control to "7" or "8." Experiment until it sounds right.

Set your amp to a clean sound. Then, add a very small amount of overdrive (just enough to make your sound "bloom"). Set your bass to "6", middle to "4" and your treble to "6." Adjust from there to where you want to be. Turn your "bright" switch on. Add a moderate amount of reverb.

Technique:

This riff is fairly easy to play. Most of it can be played using all pick-hand down strokes. Fret-hand fingerings are very simple and straightforward. The challenge is in conveying the right "attitude." You want the sound to be assertive. Be careful not to "overblow" (pick too hard) the strings because your sound will deteriorate in these ways:

-Overblowing the strings will cause them to ring sharp, therefore out of tune.

-It will sound like you're "trying too hard." Anyone practiced in the art of "cool" will tell you that trying to hard will produce the opposite of the intended effect.

-Picking harder causes the string to sound like it has less sustain. This is because the sustained portion of the tone is comparatively much softer than the initial attack. Picking softer (and setting your amp louder to compensate) will give the illusion of more sustain.

It's a good idea to listen closely to what's coming out of your amp. If it sounds right, then you are probably doing it right. Too often we can get caught up in the "right" way to do things, while forgetting that it's really only the sound we make that matters.

Look at the last measure before the repeats (Measure 20). This is the part that your non-guitar-playing pals will think is cool. Don't be too overly concerned about the notes here. This is more like a sound effect. Take your first finger and "drag" it down the string while picking really fast. Gnarly, dude!

Tubing! - Guitar 2

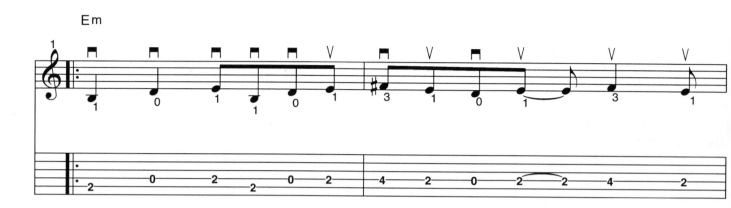

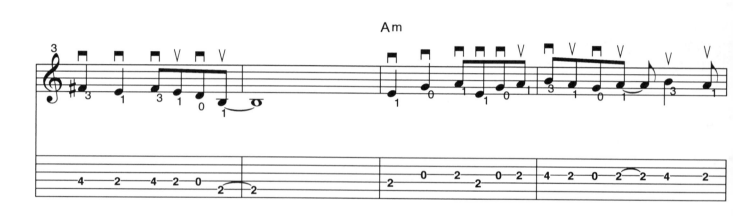

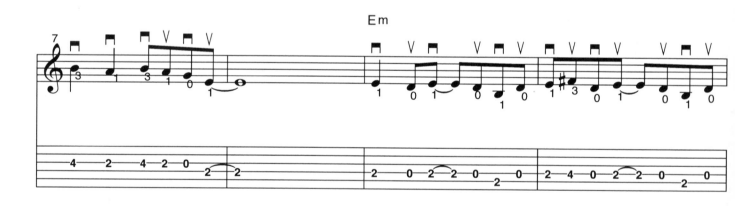

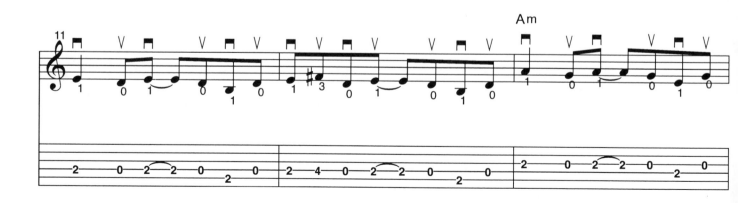

Over at the Intersection - Guitar 1
Tips on playing this riff

Tone:

Set your amp to a basic clean tone. Your tone controls should be around their mid point (check the graphic at the bottom of the page for suggested settings) as a starting point. From there you can adjust to taste. You'll likely discover that in this example, conservative settings will probably work better. This is especially true when playing with a live band. Leave the bright switch off. Add a hint of reverb if you like but it is not crucial. Set your guitar's volume and tone controls to "10" and select the bridge+middle pickups (or neck+bridge on a two-pickup guitar). If your guitar's bridge pickup is a humbucker, you may want to turn the volume back to around "8", just enough to thin out the sound.

Technique:

Pick-hand:

You'll use mostly down-strokes for this because you never go fast enough where a mix of down and up strokes are required to play it fast enough. All the notes are played two at a time. Each pair of notes are played on adjacent strings (the strings are always next to each other). When picking, place your pick on the lower (thicker) string, and pick "through and past" the higher string so that each stroke sounds both notes. The tablature in this part will show you which strings are picked. If you're having trouble isolating the two strings, you can pick "through" the two strings, and use the next string as an "anchor" to stop your pick. For example, if you play strings 5 (A) and 4 (D) together then you can pick "in to" (but not through) the 3 (G) string as a way of stopping the pick. This is an easy way to clean up your technique by preventing unintended strings from ringing.

Fret-hand:

This is a good example of "fragmented" chords. In the notation, I gave chord symbols, but not fretboard diagrams. I did this because I felt that giving the fretboard diagrams might mislead the reader in to thinking you have to finger the entire chord where it's much easier to simply finger the notes indicated. When I play the first measure I think "C chord" even though I am only playing fragments of the chord. That's because the overall sound is like a C chord. The tablature shows which frets to play while the numbers next to the notes give the fret-hand fingerings. Try them as is. After a little practice, the fingerings indicated will give you a nice smooth transition from one pair of notes to the next. It should sound easy. With practice, it will be.

Over at the Intersection - Guitar 1

Tracks 17, 18, 19,
20, 21, 22

Over at the Intersection - Guitar 2
Tips on playing this riff

Tone:

Set your amp up in the same way you would for the Guitar 1 part. Use a fairly conservative and clean setting. Troubleshoot your tone (if needed) in the way described for Guitar 1. On your guitar, you can either use the neck pickup alone, neck+middle or neck+bridge; Depending on what sounds best (in the recording, the neck pickup was used alone). Guitar 1 uses mostly low notes played in pairs, while Guitar 2 uses chords played in the higher register. The range of the notes in each part (low notes in Guitar 1, high notes in Guitar 2) is enough to keep each part distinct.

Technique:

Throughout this part you're strumming chords on the top four strings: 4 (D),3 (G),2 (B) and 1 (E). You may want to use this example to practice your pick-hand "aim", strumming only the strings you need. This may take a little time at first. Listen closely to your sound and use that as a way of gauging whether you're doing it right (good sound=probably right, bad sound=practice a little more). I find it really useful to "internalize" any rhythm pattern I am working on. In something like this, I usually like to listen to it a lot, then try either singing the pattern, or tapping it with my fingers on a tabletop. Once I have that part of it strong, it's much easier to transfer to guitar. From there I practice it until I have a flow. When I am doing this rhythm, my pick-hand is moving in a constant up-and-down motion. The pick is either scratching the strings in time, or sounding the chord. By listening to the example, you'll get the idea.

Over at the Intersection - Guitar 2

Tracks 17, 18, 19,
20, 21, 22

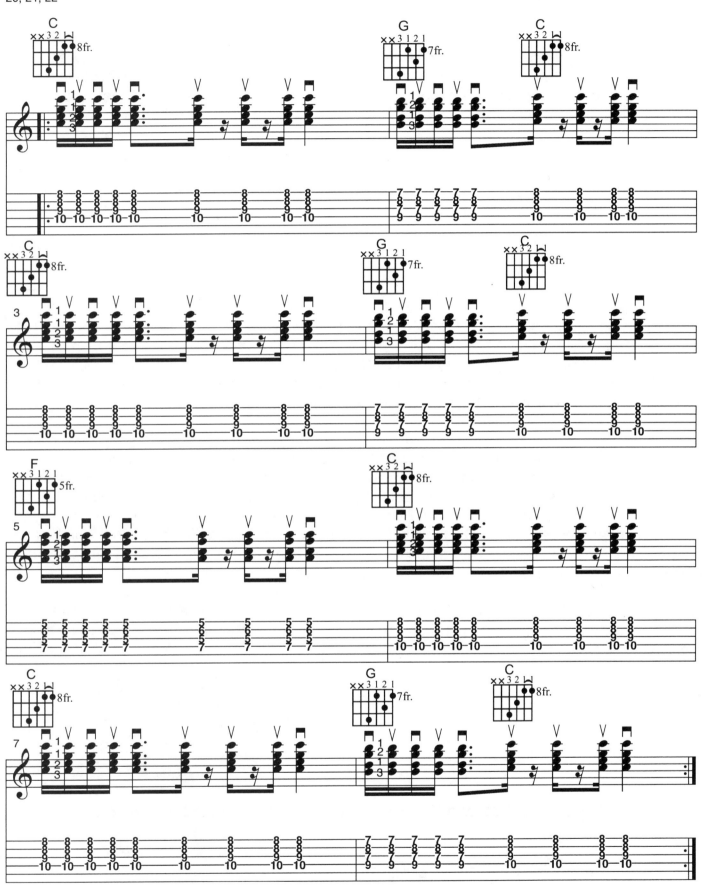

It's Getting Near Don
Tips on playing this riff:

Tone:

This tone is what guitarists in the late 60's called "psychedelic." Sometimes it was even called "Heavy Metal", but that name eventually became associated with a much heavier guitar tone. Use your guitar's neck pickup alone. Turn your guitar's volume up to "10", but then turn the "tone" control down to around "5" or "6."

Set your amp to it's overdrive channel and set the "drive" (or "gain" as it's called sometimes) to "7." Too much distortion and you lose the guitar tone and all you hear is mush. The graphic shows an example of how to set the controls. Overall, you want to accentuate the midrange part of your guitar sound as much as you can; Almost as if your amp was coming through a small tube. If your amp has a "presence" knob, set it to "0."

Technique:

The Chords:
The chords in this are a little out of the ordinary. Most of the time when we play power chords (rock chords using an overdriven amp sound), we play on two or three adjacent strings. Here, every chord is played on strings 6(E), 5(A) and 3(G). That means that we have to mute the 4(D) string along the way. To do this, I lean my fret-hand 3rd finger (which is playing the 5th string) against the 4th just enough to dampen any note that might accidentally sound.

The Notes:
After playing the chords we switch gears a little bit to play the single notes that punctuate the riff. Use a much smaller pick stroke to play the single notes so that you're hitting the string you want, and no other ones. Note that the next to last note of each phrase has a squiggly line and the marking "vib" next to it. This means vibrato. A Rock Guitar vibrato is actually a series of string bends done one after another in time. The motion is much like the way you use a doorknob. I found that to get it smooth, I had to listen closely to the sound coming from my amp, and keep adjusting my hand motions so that it sounds the way I want. A smooth vibrato takes time to develop.

At the end of the phrase, we play what we call a "crescendo" (most musical words come from Italian). Start soft, then gradually play each chord a little louder. This makes the music a little bit more dramatic.

It's Getting Near Don

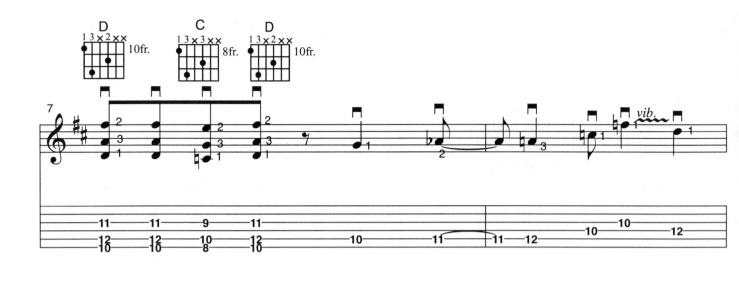

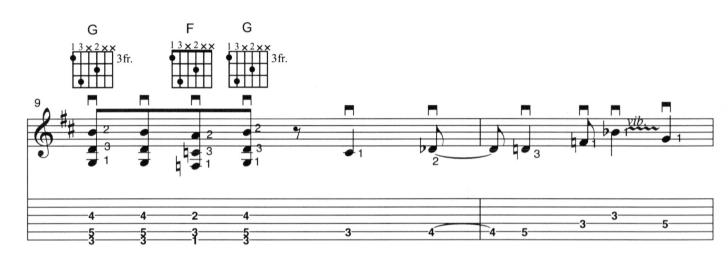

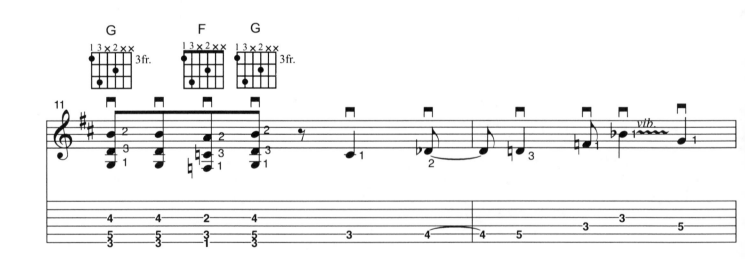

28

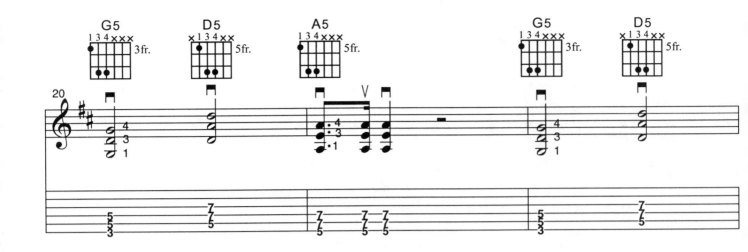

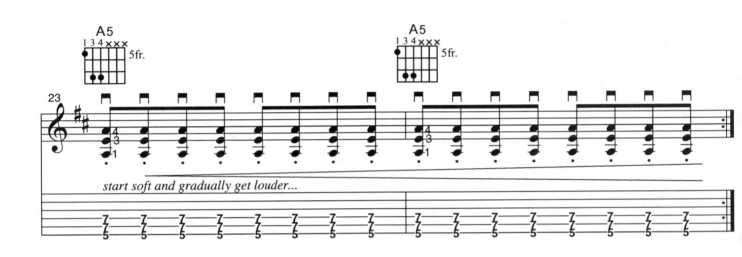

start soft and gradually get louder...

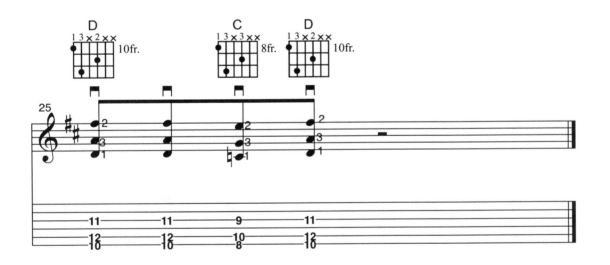

This page has been left blank to avoid awkward page turns.

More Cowbell

Tips on playing this riff

Tone:

Sometimes your guitar can be like an actor in a play. If the lyrics are telling a tragic story (like Romeo and Juliet), then your guitar tone can reflect the mood. Use your guitar's bridge pickup, and back off your tone control (on the guitar) to around "8" or "9." Set your amp as shown here. Note that a lot of midrange is used. Add a hint of reverb to give the sound a "misty air" quality.

Pick softer than normal, but turn the amp up a little to compensate. Doing this will increase the sustain of your notes without adding distortion. If you pick the string hard, the attack is very sharp but the note will die away quickly. Picking softer means that there will be a less dramatic drop in volume of the note after it's struck.

Technique:

Note the picking pattern is the same with each set of four notes: "down, down, down, up" (as shown). It is not essential that it's picked in this way, but I found it to be the smoothest. There are many places where the open "G" string is sounded. Try your best to allow that string to ring out unrestrained while playing the other notes. Standing your fret-hand fingers up will help you avoid muting it accidentally.

The "One-Finger-at-a-Time" technique:
One of the hardest things to learn is training your fingers to switch chords quickly. This example is great practice for what I call the "One-Finger-at-a-Time" technique. In the first measure, lift your 3rd finger after sounding the 3rd note (allowing the "G" string to ring). Place that same 3rd finger on the 3rd fret "E" string, immediately move your 2nd finger from 2nd fret "D" string to 2nd fret "A" string. In the third measure, place only your 1st finger on the first note, then the 3rd finger for the second note, placing each finger right before it is sounded. This avoids the need to place all your fingers at once on the chord (much more difficult, and in this case, not necessary). Keep moving your fingers in the same manner from one chord to the next. Most of the time you will find that only small moves are necessary. Read this paragraph a few times and follow the directions exactly. It may feel tedious at first, but will pay off in the long run.

More Cowbell

Tracks 26, 27, 28

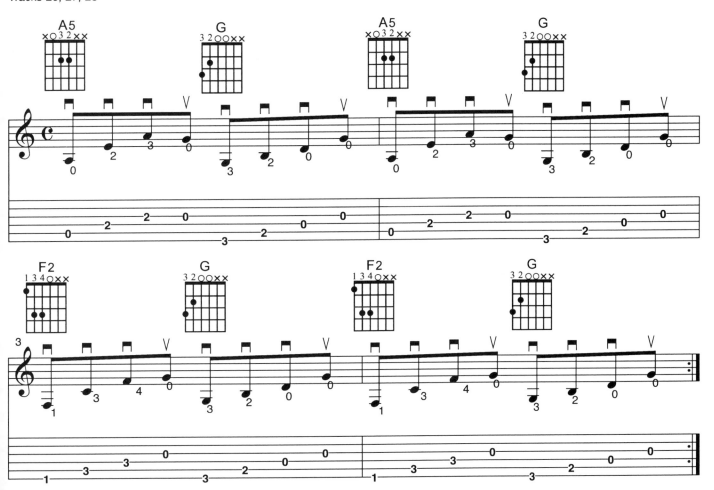

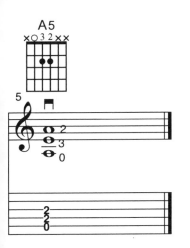

This page has been left blank to avoid awkward page turns.

Lift Your Head Higher
Tips on playing this riff

I play better when I have an image in my head of what the music would sound like. Sometimes it helps to imagine what a movie would look like if the music I am playing were the soundtrack. This example makes me think of a "Rock Parade" (if such a thing exists); A majestic, flag waving affair, but with guitars, drums, lasers and special effects rather than trumpets, baton-twirling and floats. Thinking about how a song makes you feel is important. If the sound you make causes you to feel a certain way, that is important to pay attention to and nuture. If you can convey that feeling to others through your playing, so much the better. To tell the truth, the very reason I play guitar at all is the hope that I convey my feelings through music. To do that successfully communicates at a level much deeper than any words I've found.

Tone:

Set your guitar's volume and tone controls to "10." Set the pickup selector to the bridge pickup. The amp should be set to the "drive" channel. Note that the sound in the recording is not distorted, but very slightly overdriven. There is a lot of "body" to the sound (lots of midrange tone quality). When setting up this tone, play chords very hard and see if you hear the high frequency "buzz" that usually goes with overdrive or distortion. If you can hear that "buzz", then your "drive" control (sometimes called "gain") is set too high. You should hear almost none of that "buzzing." When set properly, your guitar will sound as if you're playing thru the clean channel if you strum at a medium to medium-soft volume. If you hit the chords harder you will hear a very slight "grind" in the tone. Success here is in the subtleties.

Technique:

In the first half (measures 1-4), rest your pick-hand against the strings you're playing just slightly. Each note should sound clearly, but won't sustain past a short "thunk" sound. This is called "palm mute." In the second half (measures 5-12), release the palm mute so that each chord can ring openly. Strum hard. Use a downstroke for each chord. Be sure that the open "D" string sounds clearly for each chord (also, make sure that the low "E" and "A" strings are not ringing). The chord diagrams, tablature and fingering annotations will show you everything you need to know about how to play each chord.

35

Lift Your Head Higher

Tracks 29, 30, 31

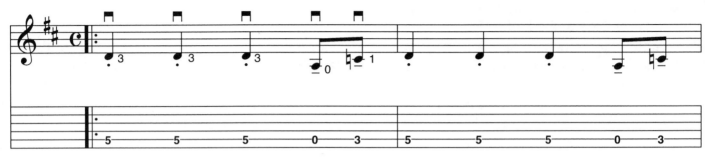

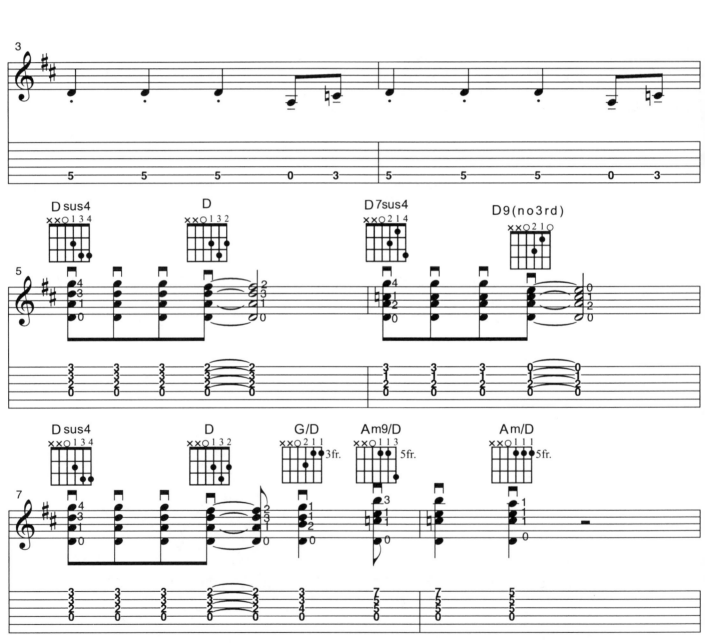

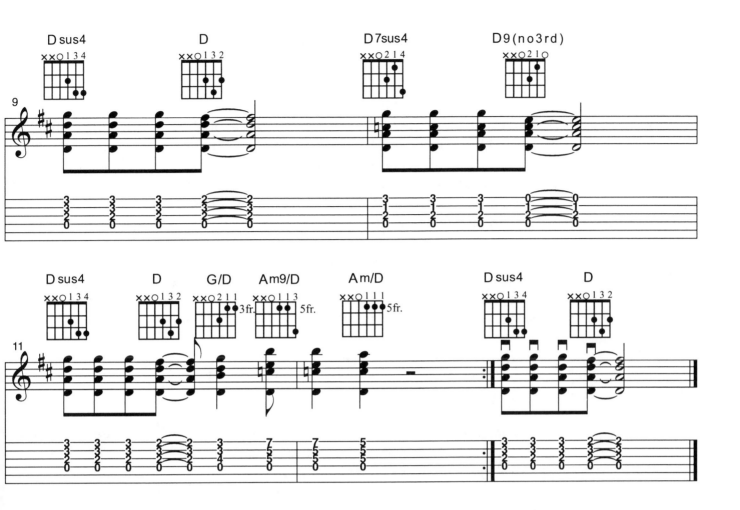

Shallow Violet

Tips on playing this riff

Tone:

In the early days of Rock & Roll guitar tone, distortion was the result of early guitar amps being punished beyond their capability; Much like driving a car with gas pedal floored all the time. Amp makers were striving for an ever-cleaner sound reproduction. Somewhere along the line, guitarists began to assert that the overdriven quality of an amp pushed beyond its limits was actually a desirable quality, provided they could play more than two concerts without the thing melting a hole through the floor. They even kicked holes in their speakers just to get "that sound."

There is a famous amp maker in the UK that got it's start by making replicas of a famous American brand. Because components were not available, he replaced some (resistors, tubes, diodes, etc.) with the closest he could find. The result was an amp that was much louder and distorted much more easily than it's American counterpart. This amp went on to become the cornerstone of the late sixties/early seventies Classic Rock era guitar tones.

Go to almost any music store even today, and you will hear guitarists playing riffs much like this one (though not exactly the same).

Turn your guitar's tone and volume all the way up to "10." Select your bridge pickup. Set your amp to a fairly hot overdrive tone. Start with your gain control set to "7", then adjust to taste. To set your amp's tone controls, start with your Bass on "5", Middle on "7" and Treble on "4." From there, re-adjust until it sounds right to you. The sound should be fairly hot and overdriven, but not "fuzzy." You should be able to hear all the notes clearly.

Technique:

The first half of this riff is played entirely on your 4th (D) and 3rd (G) strings. Practice placing your pick on the 4th (D) string and strumming across only to the next string (stop after your pick crosses the 3rd string). With each stroke of the pick you are playing two notes together. Next practice placing silence between each stroke. With an overdriven guitar tone, everything you do will sound exaggerated though your amp. The slightest movement of your fingers across the strings can produce an unpleasant "wheezing" sound through the amp. Therefore, placing silence in between each stroke takes practice. The commas in the notation suggest where to place the silence.

Your fret-hand uses a technique sometimes called "half-barre", where one finger covers more than one string, but not all six strings. It is not essential to play it this way, but I think it's much easier once your fingers become practiced at that technique. Your fret-hand fingers lay flat against the strings to be played, instead of what we normally do (standing the fingers straight up on the fretboard).

Shallow Violet

Tracks 32, 33, 34

Giving You the Business - Guitar 1
Tips on playing this riff

Tone:

Here we are going for a fairly gritty, mean rhythm guitar sound. We want enough distortion so that the chords "buzz" a little when you hit them. The drive channel will need plenty of gain. You may want to turn the "bass" control down a bit to ensure the sound doesn't "woof" too much. Start with the settings shown, then adjust to taste.

Use your guitar's "bridge+middle" pickup setting (or both pickups on if you only have two pickups). Doing this usually produces a funkier sound that "honks" more. To me the bridge pickup by itself makes more a "barking" sound where the neck pickup by itself "sings" more. Combinations of pickups tend to widen the possibilities quite a lot. I think it's worthwhile spending time getting to know how the pickup settings affect your tone. Boy, this is difficult using words to describe guitar sounds!

Technique:

Use downstrokes for each chord and rhythm. The chords seem to come out more clearly that way. Practice placing your pick just above your 5th (A) string before playing the chord. Eventually that becomes automatic. It makes for good "aim", and clearer, punchier tone. Practice sounding each chord, then lifting your fret-hand fingers just slightly between each chord. Placing a small amount of silence between each chord also makes it sound punchier still. Listen to track 33 (Guitar 1 only) and notice how there is a space (silence) between each chord. Now listen to track 32. Note how the silence makes each chord more like an "event."

Measure lines in the music are like mile markers on a road. In this case, the phrase starts on the last 8th note of the previous measure. This is called a "pickup." Don't make the mistake of trying to use the measure lines as marker for where to start or stop practicing. Doing that tends to "chop up" the phrase in a way that might make it feel awkward. Think of it this way:

"Can you tell? Me how to get to Main Street." This reads awkward right?

"Can you tell me how to get to Main Street?" This makes much more sense. The only difference is how you phrase it. Music is much the same way.

Giving You the Business - Guitar 1

Tracks 35, 36, 37,
38, 39, 40

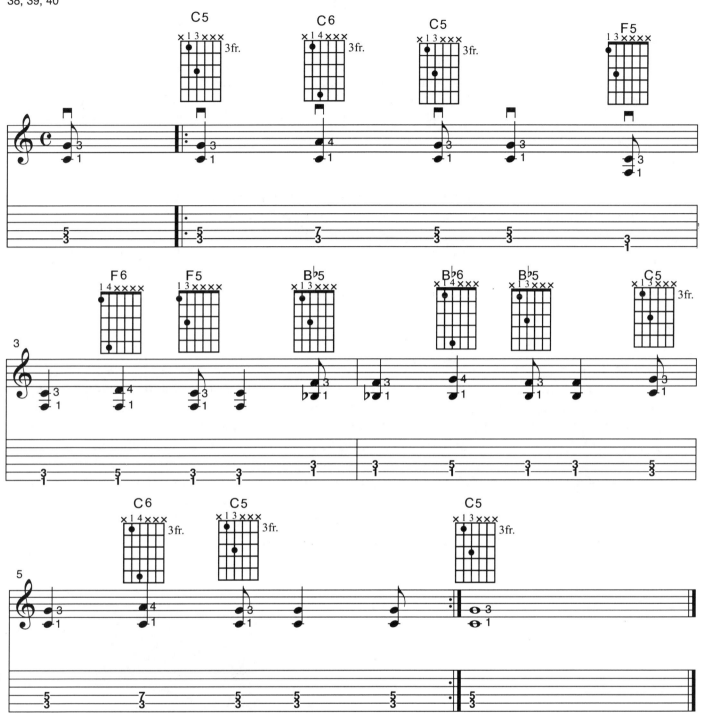

Giving You the Business - Guitar 2
Tips on playing this riff

Tone:

As you can see, the amp settings here are the same as the ones used for guitar 1. The sound is quite different. Here, the guitar is set to the neck pickup only. This makes it sing just a little more. Pickup settings, amp settings and your technique will all affect the tone you get. Play the notes fairly hard to get a sharper, tougher sound. Notice how playing harder will make the guitar a little louder but also sharper in tone. Don't play too hard though. Doing that will cause the strings to play slightly out of tune.

There is truth to the old adage, "A great guitarist can get great tone from even the worst of gear." Any good electric guitarist understands the subtleties of how their technique interacts with the setting on the amp and guitar. It's all about how it sounds coming from the amp. If you're ever wondering if you're using the right technique, listen to the sound. If it sounds right, it probably is.

Use the neck pickup, overdrive the amp, and play fairly hard.

Technique:

Here, you're strumming the top three strings to play the little chord; A higher voicing of C7 in measure 1. Next, you're playing a little blues riff starting in the last 8th note in measure two (called a pickup) over the F7 chord in measure 2. In measure 3, you're strumming a high B♭7 chord (same thing as measure one, but lower on the neck). Finally you play a blues riff over the C7. Notice that measures 3 and 4 are the same thing as measures 1 and 2, but *where* you play it is different.

It's good to know in your head what chord is happening underneath while you play something. That way, you can apply the same ideas even if you juggle the chords around and play the riffs in different places on the neck. As long as the notes fit with the chord, it should work. The best reason to learn things in this book is to use the ideas in your own way to develop your own sound!

Giving You the Business - Guitar 2

Tracks 35, 36, 37,
38, 39, 40

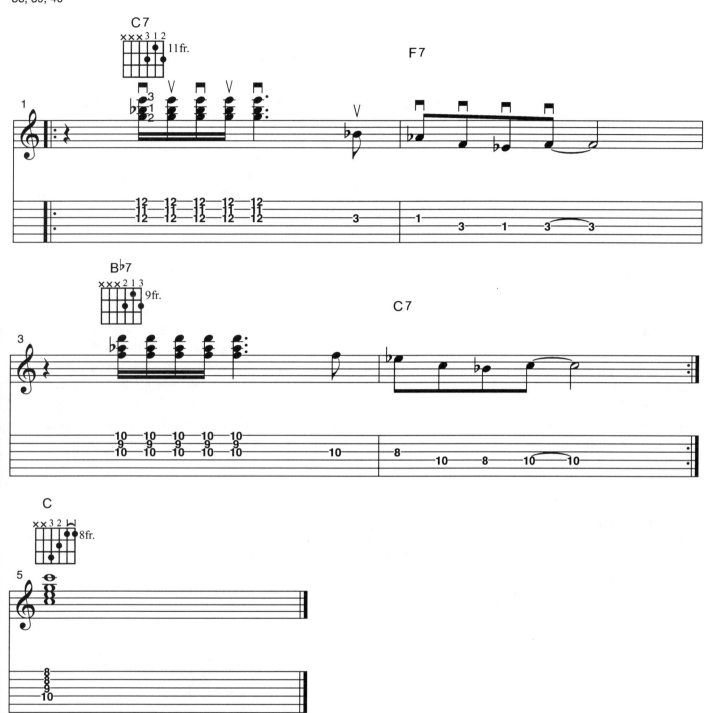

Sour Condo in Pittsburgh

Tips on playing this riff

Tone:

This is the classic 70's Southern Rock tone. Set your guitar's volume and tone controls to "10." If it's a strat-like guitar (with 3 pickups and a 5-way pickup selector), use the middle+bridge setting. If it's a two-pickup model, use either the neck+bridge setting, or bridge pickup alone. Pick closer to the bridge, but not so much that it "twangs."

On your amp, start with a small amount of overdrive. You can experiment with using your amp's lead channel, or an overdrive stompbox, whichever sounds best. You don't want the distortion to add any "buzz" to the notes. Rather, the overdrive is simply used to create thickness around the note. Starting with the amp's tone controls set to their mid-point position (usually around "5" or so), turn the treble down to around "3.5" or "4" and turn the "middle" up to around "6" or "7."

Technique:

Pick the notes pretty hard. You're going for a relaxed, funky "quacky" sound. The lowest and highest notes in each measure should also be the loudest. Pick them a little harder than the others. Try the picking and fingering markings as they are written. If they are different than what you've been doing, it might feel awkward at first. Usually, I pick downbeats with downstrokes because it helps me keep the feel more relaxed and natural. This riff does have several places though, where it's much easier to play the other way around. The high notes on the "B" string are always indicated as up strokes. Try it that way and see how it works. As always, make the sound coming from your amp the priority, and your means of judging "right technique" and "wrong technique."

Music:

This riff is divided into four phrases. Each one starts the same way but ends a little differently each time. Actually, it follows an "ABAC" form. The first and third riffs (The "A" riffs) are exactly the same, where the second ("B") and fourth ("C") are different from each other and from the "A" riffs. When a riff is repetitive like this, it can be a challenge to focus enough to play the right parts in the right order. For me, it's always helpful to think "ABAC" when I play this.

Sour Condo in Pittsburgh

Tracks 41, 42, 43

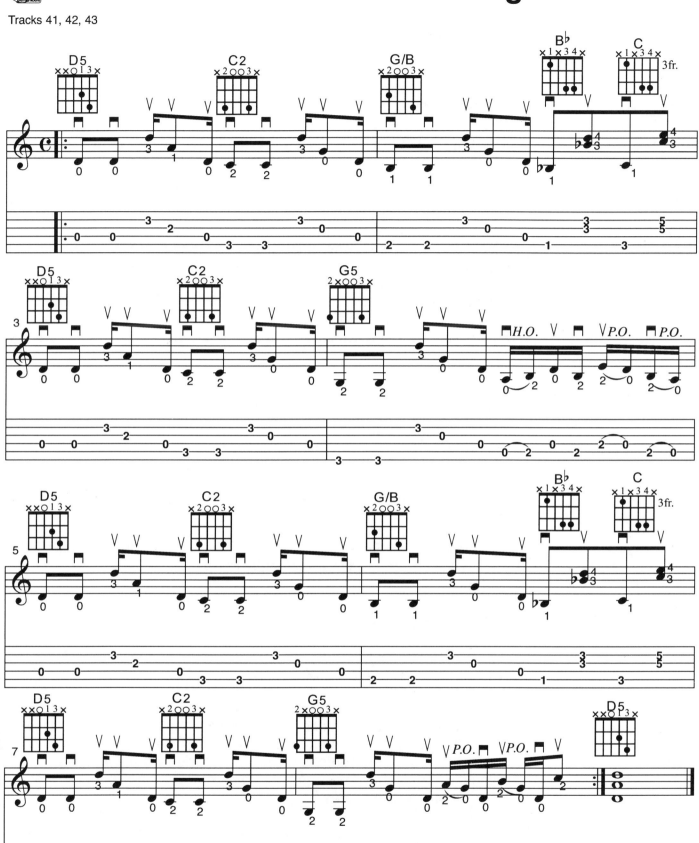

45

Glossary of Terms

◼   Downstroke with a pick

∨   Upstroke with a pick

Arpeggio   Notes of a chord played one at a time.

Bass   The lower sounding portion of your sound. Your thick (wound) strings are called bass strings. Your amp will often have a "bass" control knob.

Bridge   Located on the body of the guitar. Used as a "fulcrum" point for the vibrating part of the string, along with the nut.

Distortion   Distortion is what happens when you push an amplifiers pre-amp past it's capability. Certain types of distortion create an aggressive rock guitar sound. Many guitar amps will create distortion, especially if it has a "lead channel" with "gain" and volume controls. Manipulating the gain and volume knobs will create different types of distortion. There are many stompboxes available that will imitate the sound of distortion. Also, see "Overdrive"

Double-stop   Two notes played together.

EQ   Short for "equalizer." EQ is the generic term for any electronic device that manipulates high, middle and low tones in a variety of ways. Your bass, middle and treble controls are simple EQ devices.

Fingerboard   Located on the neck of the guitar. This is the flat surface on the neck where the frets are located. The strings rest slightly above the fingerboard.

Fret-hand   This is the hand with which you hold down notes on the fingerboard, sometimes called "fretting." Most, but not all, guitarists fret with their left hand. This term is used to avoid confusion.

Frets   Small, flat wires on the fingerboard. Place your fret-hand fingers slightly behind a fret to sound a note.

Humbucker   A type of electric guitar pickup. Its name comes from the design which reduces electronic hum. Usually larger than a single-coil. Produces a louder, fatter tone.

Measure   Music notation contains "measure lines" which act much like mile markers on a highway. Rather than dividing music into phrases, the measure line shows you how many beats have gone by, using rhythms as a way of measuring time. The "time signature" tells you how many beats are in between the measure lines.

Middle   The middle portion of your sound. Your amp will often have a "middle" control knob.

Neck   Located between the headstock and the body. The fingerboard and frets are located on the neck.

Nut   Located at the top of the guitar's neck. Used as a "fulcrum" point for the vibrating part of the string, along with the bridge.

Overdrive	In the early days of rock and roll, amplifiers were not loud enough to compete with drum sets unless they were driven past their maximum out put, usually to the point where they were "overdriven." Since these were tube devices, the "overdriven" quality was (and is) considered a desirable tonal characteristic. That became part of what is considered the signature rock and roll guitar tone. Today there are many devices that imitate that sound without stressing your guitar amp. Some are built in to the amp, while others come in little metal cases that plug in between your guitar and amplifier, called a "stompbox."
Pick-hand	This is the hand with which you hold your pick and strum chords. Most, but not all, guitarists pick with their right hand. This term is used to avoid confusion.
Pickup	A magnetic device used like a microphone for electric guitar. Uses magnets to convert string vibration into electric current. Many electric guitars have more than one pickup because the placement of the pickup under the string will influence tone. The most common pickups are humbucker and single-coil.
Pickup Selector	A device (usually a switch) that controls which pickup, or combination of pickups, is active.
Position Markers	Usually dots, squares, or other designs. Used as a visual aid in locating fret position.
Reverb	Electronic device that imitates the sound of a large hall.
Single-coil	A type of electric guitar pickup. Produces a bright, thin sound.
Stompbox	An electronic device that plugs between your guitar and amp. Called a stompbox because it rests on the floor in front of you, and you "stomp" on it to turn it on. They are used to create different types of effects: distortion, overdrive, reverb, echo, tremolo and almost anything else you can think of.
Tablature	A method of guitar notation where 6 lines represent each guitar string (the bottom line is the low E string, the top line is the high E string. Numbers on each line are used to represent which fret on which string is to be used.
Tailpiece	Used as an anchor point for the end of each string.
Time Signature	Located at the beginning of the music notation, it tells you how many beats are in between the measure lines
Treble	The high portion of your sound. The thin (unwound) strings are called treble strings. Your amp will often have a "treble" control knob.
Tremolo	Some amplifiers have an electronic tremolo effect. It usually has two controls: "depth" and "rate." Imagine asking a robot to grab your volume control and turn up, then down, then up and down (then keep going till you tell it to stop). The depth control tells it how far to turn the volume control in each direction (loudest vs. softest). The "Rate" control tells it how fast. Commonly used in sixties surf and pop styles.

Jon Finn

Jon Finn has taught in the guitar department at Berklee College of Music for many years, currently holding the title of Professor. His band, "Jon Finn Group" gained worldwide acclaim from their concert tours and CD releases (Don't Look so Serious - Legato Records 1994 and Wicked - SEP Records 1998). In 1996, Jon began writing a monthly instructional column for the nationally published Guitar magazine. His band, his teaching and his published pieces have all been dedicated to the advancement of modern electric guitar. He's performed/recorded with renowned guitarists John Petrucci (Dream Theater), Vinnie Moore, Andy Timmons and Steve Morse (Dixie Dregs), New York Voices, Collin Raye, Debbie Reynolds and a long list of other artists. Jon plays guitar with the Boston Pops Orchestra, performing in concert halls all over the world. His recording credits with them include two Grammy nominated recordings, "The Celtic Album" (1997 BMG Classics) and "The Latin Album" (1999 BMG Classics), three other CDs with The Pops ("My Favorite Things", "A Splash of Pops", "Sleigh Ride") and "The NFL Theme Song" (2004). He has also played in many contemporary national touring musical theater productions such as "Rent", "Mamma Mia!", "Aida", "Joseph and the Amazing Technicolor Dreamcoat", "Copacabana" and many others. Check out Jon's other books, "Advanced Modern Rock Guitar Improvisation", "One Guitar, Many Styles", and "Blues/Rock Improvisation" which are also available from Mel Bay. Visit www.jonfinn.com.